A LITTLE
STYLE
BOOK

A LITTLE STYLE BOOK

SCANDINAVIAN
COUNTRY

JoAnn Barwick and
the editors of *House Beautiful*
Text by Norma Skurka

Clarkson Potter/Publishers   New York

Text copyright © 1991, 1995 by Norma Skurka
Photographs copyright © 1991, 1995 by Hearst Corp. *Photographs in Scandinavian Country by Laurie Dickson, Peo Eriksson, Finnish Tourist Board, Kari Haavisto, Lars Hallen, Dana Hyde, Thibault Jeansen, Lars Kaslov, Knut Langeland, Elyse Lewin, Carl Mannerfelt, Tom McCavera, H. J. Orslev, Bent Rej, Paul Ryan, Marc Sadan, Schroder, Michael Skott, Joe Standart, William P. Steele, Jan Tennek, Paul Wistman, and Bo Zaunders*

Published by Clarkson N. Potter, Inc., 201 East 50th Street, New York, New York 10022. Member of the Crown Publishing Group.

Random House, Inc. New York, Toronto, London, Sydney, Auckland

CLARKSON N. POTTER, POTTER, and colophon are trademarks of Clarkson N. Potter, Inc. Originally published by Clarkson N. Potter, Inc. in 1991

Manufactured in China

Design by Renato Stanisic

Library of Congress Cataloging-in-Publication Data
Barwick, JoAnn.
   Scandinavian country / JoAnn Barwick and the editors of House beautiful ; text by Norma Skurka.—1st ed.
      p.   cm.—(A little style book)
   1. Decoration and ornament, Rustic—Scandinavia. 2. Country furniture—Scandinavia. I. Skurka, Norma. II. House beautiful. III. Title. IV. Series.
   NK147.B37 1995
   745.4'4948—dc20   95-2557
                                                         CIP
ISBN 0-517-88460-7

10 9 8 7 6 5 4 3 2 1

Revised Edition

CONTENTS

INTRODUCTION

Crowning the European continent, Scandinavia occupies a unique position in both the world at large and the world of design. It is a land of extremes in climate and geography, where ancient tradition exists alongside modern innovation. In this century, Scandinavian design has come to represent clean-lined objects crafted with consummate skill. The contemporary furniture of Denmark, Sweden, and Finland is world renowned and considered among the supreme achievements of 20th-century design.

Less well known but just as delightful to our eyes are the period country furniture and folk arts of these Nordic lands. Domestic items are often unique and original, created in a labor of love and marked by the personal stamp of the maker. In Scandinavian hands, even plebian objects take on patrician status.

Sweden, Denmark, Norway, Finland, and Iceland, the loose confederation of nations that comprise Scandinavia, are as varied in terrain as their people are in temperament.

Like cousins in a close-knit family who have gone their separate ways, the nations' customs are related but each one is individual in spirit. The common bonds shared by all the Nordic artisans are a love of nature, a respect for natural materials, and an innate sense of proportion and scale.

Sweden's Gustavian style, developed in the 18th century, is Scandinavian design at its most sophisticated and worldly. Inspired by the French Louis XVI, Gustavian neoclassicism perfectly expressed the Scandinavian penchant for refinement and restraint. In its provincial variations, it is responsible for the most enduring and charming of all Scandinavian country styles. Gustavian manor houses spread to Denmark, where they coexisted with that country's indigenous residence, a thatch-roofed dwelling that had changed very little since medieval times.

Norway preserves the raw energy and primitive origins of Scandinavian design. Thanks to a mountainous terrain, Norway has always been hard to invade and easy to defend against stylistic incursion. The Norse artistic legacy touched upon building techniques, woodworking, weaving, and carving, the same skills responsible for the sturdy ships that navigated the then-known world. Finnish design reflected that country's harsher climate and economic conditions. Wood, Finland's chief resource, was also its primary means of poetic expression and Finns utilized every part of the tree, fashioning the bark into woven baskets and hewing trunks into log buildings and furniture.

The Nordic emphasis on original beauty and honest workmanship is, of course, a harbinger of modern design and explains why it sprang so naturally to the Scandinavian imagination. In few places on earth do age-old handicrafts merge so seamlessly into contemporary design. The gentle decoration, the lively colors, the subtle hand-painting—all of these elements speak to us about sentiments we find missing in modern times and appreciate in Scandinavian Country.

PRECEDING PAGES: *On a misty morning, the panorama of Jutland's hayfields, bordered by beech woods and barns, is a picture of Danish harmony.*

LOOKING
OUTSIDE

SCANDINAVIANS *live close to nature. Their homeland in the far north is one of the few places on earth still free of visual and industrial pollution, and Scandinavians are passionate about their role as custodians of this last unspoiled frontier. At every bend in the road, the countryside beckons with views worthy of an artist's paintbrush. Fishing villages, lighthouses, gardens, farms, cottages, and mansions slip in and out of sight, framed by a patchwork of field and forest, endless seacoast or boundless sky. The landscape changes abruptly among these five separate nations, ranging from the majestic mountains and sparkling fjords of Norway to the docile, pastoral seacoasts of Denmark, from the verdant meadows of Sweden to the island-dotted tundra of Finland and Iceland.*

The architecture, too, bears a distinct national stamp. If one building type can epitomize a country's architectural personality, Sweden's romantic lusthuses *perfectly capture the Scandinavian love affair with summer. These tiny open-air pavilions were built around the turn of the century* solely to enjoy the last rays of the sun on long June nights. In Denmark, the rambling whitewashed barns sheltered by deep thatch roofs resemble nothing as much as a medieval village in miniature and give the landscape a sense of permanence. Norwegian bonders, the farm families in remote mountain valleys, lavish their granaries, the stabburs, with carving and paint: they are the pride of the farm and reflect a family's social standing in the community.

Finns cherish their island hideaways, although these may be little more than a one-room cabin. Because the islands of the Finnish archipelago are too numerous to count, a family can own their own. The rewards of living on nature's doorstep, savoring the solitude, relishing the absence of noise and pollution, outweigh the inconveniences. Most Scandinavians would not have it any other way.

PRECEDING PAGES: *A thatch-roofed cottage on the Danish fishing island of Fanø sports sunny yellow walls and a jaunty green door.*

VIEWS

LEFT: *The geometric design on the door of a very ancient Danish farmhouse in the Frilandsmuseet, an open-air museum, looks so modern it could have been painted yesterday.* **PRECEDING PAGES:** *Short Nordic summers lure everyone outdoors to enjoy a sunny spot, even in a meadow of wildflowers.*

A Danish farm on the island of Bjornholm has the best of views: rolling hills and the sea.

The lighthouse at Skagen, Denmark's northernmost tip, beckons sailors home to the little fishing village of Hirtshals.

Above: *The midnight sun haunts the horizon in a Finnish archipelago.*
Right: *A rowboat bobs in the stillness of a glacial lake at dusk.*

FAR LEFT: *Heddal Stavkirke is Norway's largest stave church.*
CLOCKWISE FROM TOP LEFT: *The wood tiles on an ancient stavkirke is a holdover from Viking shipbuilding crafts. A lock is fashioned from a horseshoe on the Halabrekka farm in Norway. A Finnish clocktower is topped with an onion-shaped dome.*

TID FOR
SOMMER-
MØBLER

ABOVE: *A well-weathered gate swings lazily on its hinges in Sweden.* **LEFT:** *Sturdy clapboard warehouses have lined the quays in Bergen since the 16th century, when it was a Hanseatic port.*

ABOVE: *An intrepid traveler glides over the Finnish snow on a sleigh pulled by a reindeer.* **RIGHT:** *Slender pines gracefully shoulder the burden of a Nordic winter.*

LEFT: *Few places on earth rival the majesty of Norway's mountain fjords.* **BELOW:** *Snow-filled fishing boats hibernate on the beach of the Oslo Fjord, awaiting spring.*

ABOVE: *A log-cabin hideaway was shipped to the remote Finnish island of Brännskär piece by piece.* **RIGHT:** *In Norway's mountain valleys, the roofs sprout hay like a farm boy's unruly cowlick.* **FOLLOWING PAGES:** *Country roads in Sweden reward with a visual bouquet of flowers and fences in any season.*

EXTERIORS

LEFT: *Lace curtains peep through a cottage window sheltered by a rustic thatch roof.* **PRECEDING PAGES:** *At the Frilandsmuseet in Denmark, the rosy hues of an ancient half-timbered cottage are offset by the jolly electric blue windows and door.*

The Wedberg family compound on the Swedish island of Lidingö, near Stockholm, grew over the span of a century. The main house was built in 1775; another building was added later, as the clan expanded.

A typical Scandinavian cottage is painted red and trimmed in white. Traveling along the Swedish byroads, one encounters hundreds of farmhouses that exhibit this charming country style.

Throughout Norway and Sweden, red was the traditional color of choice for most farm buildings. "Falun red," a mixture of copper pigment and linseed oil, was a popular wood preservative and also a less costly brick look-alike.

Liselund, an 18th-century estate on the Isle of Møn, is a jewel of Danish neoclassicism. Its enchantment derives from its rustic features, thatch roof, white-washed walls, and tall windows arranged with Palladian symmetry.

Above: *Odenslunda, a 200-year-old manor house in Sweden, was in ruins when its present owners found it.*
Right: *The medieval form of this Nordic farmstead has changed little over time.*

An 18th-century manor house exhibits the stately grace and simple geometry that are hallmarks of Swedish design. Most mansions are not considered complete without the central cupola.

The generous proportions of a typical Swedish country manor were meant to house an extended family and stay-over guests. Travel was arduous over wintry roads; once they arrived at their destination, friends stayed put.

An immaculate whitewashed stable, outside Aabenraa in Denmark near the German border, proudly displays its age.

ABOVE AND RIGHT: *The medieval thatch-roofed dwellings in Scandinavia give the landscape a deep sense of permanence. Thatch suits the climate well; it is warm in winter and cool in summer.* **FAR RIGHT:** *In Finland, where forests range over most of the land, log cabins are the pervasive house form.*

On Fanø island off the Jutland coast, descendants of the old sailing families compete to make their doorways unique. These colorful portals have been welcoming Danish seamen home since the 1700s.

LITTLE HOUSES

56

FAR LEFT: *The* stabbur, *or gra-nary, is the most picturesque building on a Norwegian farm.* **ABOVE LEFT AND RIGHT:** *Farmers paint their granaries or embel-lish them with carvings.* **LEFT:** *A Swedish* lusthus *is typically more refined.* **PRECEDING PAGES:** *The Swedes' open-air pavilions express their sun-loving natures.*

ABOVE: *A garden house in Denmark is the perfect spot for afternoon tea.* **LEFT:** *A crown of windows gives this* lusthus *the feeling of a miniature lighthouse.* **PRECEDING PAGES:** *The popular* lusthus, *here placed at the water's edge, is the Swedish equivalent of a gazebo.*

Top left: *A "hermit's retreat" is made of tree trunks.* **Right, above and below:** *Summerhouses range from a playful open octagon to an elegant mini-palace.* **Far right:** *This airy wood-lattice gazebo, resembling a giant aviary, was built by the grandfather of the present Swedish king for his wife.*

LOOKING INSIDE

IN the design of their interiors, Scandinavians found the way to take the stuffiness out of European formality without compromising classic beauty. Their country homes have a sense of suitability, a lack of pretension, and a touch of whimsy to delight the eye. The hallmarks we love in these homes are the sun-splashed rooms where gauzy curtains billow across the floor, where blue-and-white ginghams cover chair seats and windows, where simple rag runners accent the scrubbed pine floors. The look of a Scandinavian interior is spare but warm, with graceful furniture that is delicately proportioned. Blond wood is either left natural or painted in light pastel tones. What surprises us most about these delightful dwellings is the ingenuity and variety of their decorated interiors.

The desire for cheery light-filled spaces during the long Nordic winters explains why so many rooms are animated by color and pattern. Hand-painting is the most dazzling of the native arts. Hundreds of old houses display a bravura of faux finishes, such as glazing, pinstriping, marble-

izing, stippling, and wood graining, combined in ingenious ways. Norwegian rosemaling is an ancient peasant folk art that blanketed entire rooms in florid patterns. Taste turned to more delicate motifs during the Gustavian period, 1775 to 1810, favoring floral sprays, swags, twining ribbons, and leafy borders. The color bias also shifted away from strong, saturated primaries to sun-washed shades with the translucency of watercolors.

What comes down to us across the centuries in the Scandinavian home, whether an elegant country manor or a comfortable farmstead, is its livability. The aim of the room is not to impress but to please. In their marvelous diversity, Scandinavian homes offer something for every taste. Sophisticates will respond to the cool elegance of a Gustavian villa while fanciers of country fare will be just as enchanted by the innocent charm of a farmer's cottage.

PRECEDING PAGES: *The dining room of a 19th-century stonemason's cottage reveals the simple elegance of Danish Gustavian style.*

LIVING

ABOVE: *Marimekko's founder, Armi Ratia, furnished her country home with antiques and flea market finds.* **RIGHT:** *French doors merge the neoclassical interiors of Liselund with its parklike setting on the Danish island of Møn.* **PRECEDING PAGES:** *Colorful textiles provide the decoration in a cabin on a Finnish island.*

In Finland, the Biedermeier style arrived via Russia, bringing with it the Imperial taste for bold outlines and touches of ormolu. The use of lighter wood, however, is distinctly Scandinavian.

A family's collection of personal items—scarves, jackets, umbrellas, boots, and hats—cheerfully clutters the foyer of a restored 18th-century farmhouse outside Stockholm.

In the nonchalance of a Scandinavian sitting room, a farm table, chairs, and a handmade rocking horse seem perfectly at ease with modern white sofas.

The panels of a well-worn doorway in a Gudbrands-dalen farmhouse are painted with a fanciful tree motif. It was probably the work of an itinerant artist traveling the remote Norwegian provinces during the last century.

ABOVE: *Most furniture throughout Scandinavia is painted white to brighten the interiors. This room is a modern interpretation, done with reproductions.* **LEFT:** *Twin side chairs are plain country versions of the more formal Gustavian style.*

RIGHT: *Historically, the Norwegian living room was the center of all daytime activities. Children and household help slept in the loft, accessible by a ladder.* **PRECEDING PAGES:** *An old Norwegian slagbenk, a bench with a bed inside, still bears much of its original brilliant blue paint.*

FAR LEFT, CLOCKWISE FROM TOP LEFT: *Freshly cut field flowers are a constant presence in a Nordic home. Another key feature is light floors, either natural scrubbed pine or painted. In 1897 a country carpenter fashioned two rocking cradles and signed one of them.* **LEFT, TOP:** *A blue doorway in the Laerdal Museum illustrates Norwegian rosemaling dating from 1799.* **BOTTOM:** *Beautiful tiled stoves warmed Nordic rooms long before central heating.*

Each of Norway's provinces developed distinctive colors and designs. These lively domestic arts include a hand-painted child's rocking cradle and a decorated corner cupboard. Curtains, too, were hand-crocheted.

A suite of Gustavian parlor furniture with striped covers is painted white for summer lightness and informality in typical Swedish fashion. Beside the tall ceramic stove, family portraits line the walls.

93

RIGHT: *An unusual painted Empire daybed is updated with colorful chintz pillows and paired with rattan furniture. This one-room cottage sits a stone's throw from the Baltic seacoast of Sweden.* **PRECEDING PAGES:** *A lantern's globe and the extraordinary trompe l'oeil effects at Liselund capture Danish neoclassicism at its finest. This 19th-century mansion on the island of Møn is open to the public and worth a visit.*

Liselund's decor was inspired by the ruins of Pompeii, which had just been discovered when the manor house was begun in 1800.

A Swedish "best room" brings together furnishings that span three centuries, including a sinuous Empire side chair, a classic Biedermeier daybed and pedestal table, and two reproduction armchairs updated with striped down-filled cushions.

ABOVE: *A painted armoire and trio of rockers are part of the owner's collection of Finnish country antiques.* **RIGHT:** *Family portraits and mementos hang above an Empire writing table in a Finnish ship captain's study.*

A tapestry fire screen before a ceramic stove shares a parlor corner with a Biedermeier chair and console table. The rare wallpaper mural was exported to Finland from France in about 1830.

Isak Dinesen, the author of
Out of Africa, was raised at
Rungstedlund in Denmark.
Her childhood home is now
a working retreat for writers;
her study is kept just as
she left it. The early 20th-
century furniture exhibits
hints of "Danish modern"
still to come.

To cheer up gloomy winters, wealthy Finns brightened their homes with painted patterns. Here, the elaborately painted door of a ballroom opens onto a living room furnished with Biedermeier appointments. This ship captain's residence was the height of fashion in Kristinestad around 1900.

Blond woods with black accents are keynotes of Swedish Biedermeier. A wall cupboard mimics the bonnet top of a larger armoire. Blue-and-white is a favorite color scheme for both Swedish porcelain and, below, a Finnish parlor. A chair and armoire focus on the delicacy of Gustavian painted details. A Finnish living room exhibits the heavier Biedermeier style it imported from Imperial Russia.

Unmatched furniture, wall-paper patterns, and area rugs extend through the parlors of a country manor in Stockholm's archipelago. Over the years, several generations accumulated the furnishings, and the effect, while unplanned, is instantly pleasing.

A gallery at Rungstedlund, author Isak Dinesen's Danish home, enjoys the sheer trailing curtains that are a Scandinavian trademark. Matching Victorian pier glasses flank the open porch doorway.

A white bench with blue checked cover, a country basket, and geraniums blooming on a windowsill extend a Swedish welcome in a cottage's garden entrance.

Tall case clocks illustrate the range and whimsy of Scandinavian design. Country models were left in their natural blond woods, painted traditional white, or decorated in the livelier colors pre-

ferred in the rural provinces. Gustavian clocks featured classical motifs and an elegant gilt finish.

In the sunny whitewashed bedroom of a restored farmhouse, a half-round pine table fits neatly beneath a window; its simple lines contrast with the scalloped back of an antique daybed. The farmhouse is located in Skåne, Sweden's southernmost province.

The African collection of Baroness Blixen, better known as Isak Dinesen, flavors her study with exotica. Spears from the Masai and Somali tribes of Kenya intermingle with Danish furniture at Rungstedlund, her childhood home.

In the Gustavian style, Sweden
borrowed motifs from the
French Louis XVI but quickly
nationalized them. Classical
motifs were interpreted on mir-
rors, chairs, and cupboards as
romantic carved or painted
bows, ribbon swags, floral
wreaths, and tapering curves.

DINING

PRECEDING PAGES: *A buffet at Odenslunda in Sweden tantalizes the eye with its subtle contrasts: the cream-colored porcelain tureen and the pickled wood tones are sharpened by tart green apples and black candlesticks.* **RIGHT:** *Painting furniture white is a long-standing Nordic tradition meant to camouflage inferior wood and to make the furniture appear more grand. The dining room at Lund Gard, which has been in the same Norwegian family for 350 years, is furnished with an exuberant version of country rococo.*

126

The furniture in the Søre Høimyr farmhouse in Numedal, Norway, has been in continuous use for over a century. The vivid paint colors have worn away to a rich patina.

A country kitchen in a
Norwegian suburb is
furnished with a sturdy pine
table and an unmatched
set of dining chairs, found
by the young owners at vari-
ous times on antiquing
forays in the countryside.

ABOVE: *At the heart of the dining area of a restored Swedish cottage is an old table, first painted a bright yellow, then outlined in a darker shade.* **RIGHT:** *The dining room at Odenslunda, a Swedish manor house, features a beautiful Gustavian tiled stove and appointments of the period.*

The painting and cabinetry in this ancient Norwegian farmstead in the Gudbrands-dal Valley was probably the work of a single craftsman hired to decorate the room and make its furniture all at one time.

Norwegian farmsteads are living records of Scandinavia's most ancient crafts. A hutch cupboard, displaying a family's special china, is both intricately carved and painted in vivid, contrasting tones.

A cottage dating from the 1880s was dismantled and shipped to a Finnish island to create this inviting one-room hideaway. Although it provides only the bare necessities for living, the simplicity of the rustic furniture makes it inviting.

ABOVE AND RIGHT: *When in season, flowers fill the homes, but to compensate for short summers, furniture panels are decorated with flower garlands and bouquets.* **FAR RIGHT:** *Scandinavian armoires and cupboards are works of folk art. These fine Finnish examples were collected by Armi Ratia, Marimekko's founder.*

Half of a one-room cottage in Sweden is reserved for a dining table, surrounded by country Gustavian chairs. Touches of the owner's creative spirit—such as the floral sprays stenciled on the pine floors—greet the eye.

In the dining room at Liselund in Denmark, every surface is painted in a monochromatic scheme of faux marble. Mirrored alcoves echo the arched French doors with Palladian precision.

The charm of a Finnish farmhouse kitchen lies in its naturalness: homespun curtains, a hand-woven table runner, wooden utensils, and a bouquet of fresh greenery when flowers are out of season.

148

ABOVE: *Traditional blue-and-white china lines a wall at Skoga-holm, a restored Gustavian manor house.* **LEFT:** *The painted decoration on a cupboard exhibits the florals typical of Sweden's inland provinces.*

Inside a tiny Danish tea-house every surface sports an elegant paint treatment, from the dado and base-board to the diamond-patterned floor and even the pinstriped furniture.

151

COOKING

ABOVE: *The kitchen in an old farmhouse was updated with new cabinets and appliances.* **RIGHT:** *Kitchen utensils display Scandinavian flair.* **PRECEDING PAGES:** *This cooking fireplace was copied from a traditional Norwegian design. Cubbyholes are a modern innovation.*

With its assortment of tables and chairs for cooking, eating, or just passing time, this roomy kitchen on the tiny island of Tåtøy in Kragerø is the hub of vacation living for a family from Oslo.

A worktable holds a variety of cooking pots, copper kettles, bowls, utensils, and serving pieces in a Finnish pantry unchanged since the 18th century.

ABOVE: *Before the advent of cupboards, wall shelves provided china storage as well as a decorative accent.* **LEFT:** *Handmade butter and cheese presses, hung on wall racks or pegs, and an old-fashioned butter churn evoke nostalgia for bygone days.*

*Traditionally, domestic life
centered around the stone
cooking hearth in the Nordic
home. Guests were favored
with a berth near this major
source of winter warmth.*

ABOVE: *The kitchen of a
restored cottage captures
modern decor done in the
Danish manner.* **LEFT:**
*Antique creamware tureens
and pewter chargers are
prized possessions at Olive-
hut, a Swedish manor house
with an ancient past.*

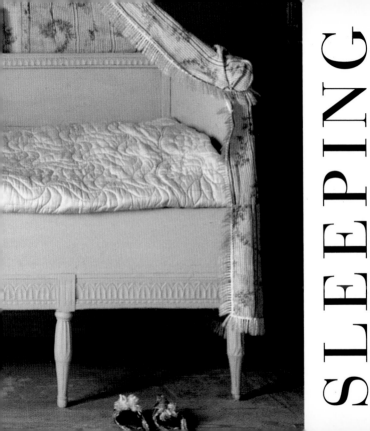

SLEEPING

PRECEDING PAGES: *A prosperous merchant in Finland was proud of his Swedish-style daybed, charmingly draped.* **RIGHT:** *The bedroom of an 18th-century Swedish manor house includes fine Gustavian pieces, such as the veneered chest of drawers, daybed, and tall case clock. Curtain fabrics reproduce documentary prints of the period.*

Sun streams through the deeply inset windows into the bedroom of a restored Swedish farmhouse. A checkerboard print bedspread and a cotton rag runner add dashes of color to the neutral earth-toned scheme.

ABOVE: *A small wood stove heats a Norwegian guest bedroom.* **RIGHT:** *An alcove bed is tucked into a nook beneath the stairs, painted a vivid blue. A bookshelf and reading lamp make it a cozy spot to curl up with a book.*

174

ABOVE: *On a console table, a gilt clock and porcelains mingle with a bouquet of old-fashioned roses.* **LEFT:** *A painted chest, oval mirror, and headboard in a child's bedroom demonstrate the simple elegance of Danish Gustavian-style furniture.*

ABOVE: *A guest bedroom at Lund Gard, Norway, is painted a bright blue; the farm has been in the same Norwegian family for 350 years.* **RIGHT:** *In a Swedish farmhouse bedroom, a bed's head- and footboard are slipcovered to match the chair fabric.*

A collector's model ships
make a fetching display atop
an old pine bureau, which
still shows traces of its original gray-blue paint. The
bedroom walls are spatter-
painted, a technique that
has been employed in
Swedish farmhouses for
more than 200 years.

Walls papered in botanical prints and paneled with green wainscoting provide a verdant counterpoint to a gingham-covered daybed in a tiny cottage on the outskirts of Nyköping, Sweden.

The imposingly carved back of a country daybed shows a Gustavian influence. It is in a restored log cabin in Kavelia, Finland, built in 1609.

Alcove beds built into the wall, an ancient design following Viking shipbuilding techniques, are still popular in Norway. This one has a cornice embellished with elaborate scrolls.

185

ABOVE: *This guest bedroom with a carved canopy bed, on the Straumen farm in Numedal, Norway, is little changed since the late 18th century.* **LEFT:** *A modern alcove bed behind glass panels borrows the hand-painted features of old Norwegian rosemaling.*

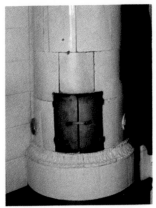

ABOVE: *Ceramic tile stoves, placed in nearly every room, were the primary heat source throughout Scandinavia until the advent of central heating.* **LEFT:** *The master bedroom in a Danish cottage is a study in simple elegance.*

189

ABOVE: *A traditional Norwegian barn was turned into a snug guest cottage.* **RIGHT:** *A restored farmhouse in Skåne, Sweden, is updated with bright hand-woven textiles and a stenciled floor. The old iron bedstead was found in the house during its renovation.*

PAINT & PATTERN

PRECEDING PAGES: *A country washstand, basin, towels, and birch-bark house slippers await farm workers in an ancient Finnish cabin, now a museum.* ABOVE LEFT AND RIGHT: *Armoires express*

Scandinavian design at its most innovative. In addition to the variety of pedimented or bonnet tops, they are invariably painted in colorful garlands, faux marbre, *or wood-grain motifs.*

ABOVE: *Folk painting on an ancient wall mural has a naïve innocence.* **RIGHT:** *Colorful hand-painted panels decorate a storage wall in an 18th-century dwelling at the Frilandsmuseet, an open-air museum near Copenhagen.*

LEFT: *A Norwegian* skap, *or hutch cupboard, is decorated with elaborate intertwining scrolls.* **FOLLOWING PAGES:** *Crafts played a major role in the life of Norwegian farm families. Ale bowls, drinking cups, chests, and boxes were embellished with folk designs and exchanged as presents on special occasions.*

200

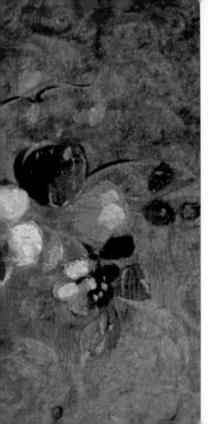

ABOVE: *Floral pattern was even used to decorate objects as small as wooden boxes.*
LEFT: *Rosemaling is Norway's most distinctive folk art. Translated literally as "rose painting," it describes the charmingly florid designs that covered both walls and furniture.*

ABOVE: *A doorway in the Laerdal Museum illustrates Norwegian rosemaling dating from 1799.* **RIGHT:** *Fanciful scenes typify mural paintings still found in old Swedish farmhouses.*

En Ridande Soldat med åtsira Urder